Robert M. De Witt

Patriotic Songster

Robert M. De Witt

Patriotic Songster

ISBN/EAN: 9783337306526

Printed in Europe, USA, Canada, Australia, Japan

Cover: Foto ©Thomas Meinert / pixelio.de

More available books at **www.hansebooks.com**

PATRIOTIC SONGSTER

NEW YORK:

ROBERT M. DE WITT,

13 FRANKFORT STREET.

DIME PATRIOTIC SONGSTER.

THE BANKS OF THE SCHUYLKILL.

On the banks of the Schuylkill so pleasant and gay,
There, bless'd with my true love, I spend the short
    day,
Where the sun shed his rays thro' the mulberry tree,
And the streams form'd a mirror for my true love
    and me.

On the spot of clover we sat ourselves down,
Not envying the greatest of monarchs that's crown'd,
My name in the sand with his fingers he drew,
And he swore by the stream he would ever prove
    true.

To which I beheld the gay pride of my fair,
I gazed on his face while he play'd with my hair,
He need not have told me his love with a sigh,
For the Schuylkill secures my dear fellow to me.

Oft times he told me the stories of love,
He would sing me a song my affections to move,
My lips were solicited, my hand gently press'd,
On the banks of the Schuylkill, Jesse was bless'd.

" Whenever we leave this enchanting retreat,"
With blushes, says he, " when next shall we meet ?"
" Next Sunday," he says, " if the weather proves
      clear,
On the banks of the Schuylkill, I'll meet you, my
      dear."

Now all these innocent pleasures are o'er,
The murmuring river can please me no more,
Since the banks of the Schuylkill have lost all
      their charms,
And the soldiers have torn my dear boy from my
      arms.

But should ever I clasp him again to my heart,
No more shall my true love and I ever part,
No more shall the wars take my true love away,
And the banks of the Schuylkill shall ever be gay.

THE SAILOR BOY'S DREAM.

In slumbers of midnight the sailor boy lay,
   His hammock swung loose at the sport of the
      wind,
But watch worn and weary, his cares flew away
   And visions of happiness danc'd on his mind.

He dreamt of his home, and his dear native bowers,
　And pleasures that waited on life's merry morn,
While memory stood side-ways, half covered with
　　flowers,
　And restored every rose, but secreted a thorn.

Then fancy, her magical pinions spread wide,
　And bade the young dreamer in ecstacy rise,
Now far, far behind him the green waters glide,
　And the cot of his forefathers blesses his eyes.

The jessamine chambers in flower o'er the hatch,
　And the swallow sings sweet from her nest in the
　　wall,
All trembling with transport he raises the latch,
　And the voices of loved ones reply to his call.

A father bends o'er him with looks of delight,
　His cheek is impearl'd with a mother's warm tear,
And the lips of the boy in the love-kiss unite,
　With the lips of the maid whom his bosom holds
　　dear.

The heart of the sleeper beats high in his breast,
　Joy quickens his pulse—all his hardships seem o'er,
And a murmur of happiness steals through his rest,
　"O God! thou hast blest me, I ask for no more."

Ah! whence is that flame, which now bursts on his
　eye?
Ah! what is that sound which now startles his ear?
'Tis the lightning's red glare, painting hell on the
　sky!

'Tis the crashing of thunder, the groan of the
sphere.

He springs from his hammock—he flies to the deck,
　　Amazement confronts him with images dire,
Wild winds and mad waves drives the vessel a wreck,
　　The masts fly in splinters—the shrouds are on fire!

Like mountains, the billows tremendously swell,
　　In vain the lost wretch calls on Mary to save,
Unseen bands of spirits are ringing his knell,
　　And the death-angel flaps his broad wings o'er
　　　　the wave.

O, sailor boy, wo to thy dream of delight,
　　In darkness dissolve the gay frost-work of bliss,
Where now is the picture that fancy touch'd bright,
　　Thy parent's fond pressure, and love-honied kiss?

O! sailor boy! sailor boy! never again,
　　Shall home, love, or kindred thy wishes repay,
Unblessed and unhonored, down deep in the main,
　　Full many a score fathom thy frame shall decay.

No tomb shall e'er plead to remembrance for thee,
　　Or redeem form or frame from the merciless surge,
But the white foam of waves shall thy winding
　　　　sheet be,
And winds in the midnight of winter thy dirge.

On beds of green sea-flowers thy limbs shall be laid,
　　Around thy white bones the red coral shall grow,

Of thy bright yellow locks threads of amber be made,
　And every part suit to thy mansion below.

Days, months, years, and ages shall circle away,
　And still the vast waters above thee shall roll,
Eartn loses thy pattern forever and aye—
　O sailor boy! sailor boy! peace to thy soul.

A LIFE ON THE OCEAN WAVE.

A life on the ocean wave!
　A home on the rolling deep!
Where scattered waters rave,
　And the winds their revels keep!
Like an eagle caged I pine
　On this dull unchanging shore;
Oh, give me the flashing brine,
　The spray, and the tempest's roar.

Once more on the deck I stand
　Of my own sweet gliding craft,
Set sail! farewell to the land:
　The gale follows far abaft.
We sport through the sparkling foam
　Like an ocean bird set free;
Like the ocean bird, our home
　We'll find far out on the sea.

The land is no longer in view,
　The clouds have begun to frown;

But with a stout vessel and crew,
    We'll say let the storm come down.
And the song of our hearts shall be,
    While the winds and waters rave,
A life on the heaving sea!
A home on the bounding wave!

A YANKEE SHIP AND A YANKEE CREW.

A Yankee ship and a Yankee crew,
    Tally hi ho! you know!
O'er the bright waves like a sea-bird flew,
    Singing hey! aloft and alow!
Her sails are spread to the fairy breeze,
The spray sparkling as thrown from her prow,
Her flag is the proudest that floats on the seas,
When homeward she's steering now.
                    A Yankee ship, &c.

A Yankee ship and a Yankee crew,
    Tally hi ho! you know!
With hearts abroad both gallant and true,
    The same aloft and alow.
The blackened sky and the whistling wind,
Foretell the approach of a gale;
And home and its joys flit over each mind.
Husbands, lovers, on deck there! a sail!
    Distress is the word, God speed them through,
        Bear a hand aloft and alow!
                    A Yankee ship, &c.

A Yankee ship and a Yankee crew !
　Tally hi ho ! you know !
Freedom defends the land where it grew,
　We're free aloft and alow !
Bearing down is a ship in regal pride,
Defiance floating at each mast-head ;
She's wrecked, and the one bears that floats along-
　　side,
The stars and stripes that's to victory wed,
　Ne'er strikes to a foe while the sky is blue,
　Or a tar's aloft and alow.

YANKEE GIRL TO HER LOVER.

Go, friend of my bosom, the trumpet's shrill cry
　Has summon'd the soldier to arms ;
With patriot valor each bosom beats high,
　And Freedom her votaries warms.

Shall I, while my country is bleeding recline
　On the bosom of indolent ease !
No ! no ! in her cause even thee I resign,
　Though naught but thy presence can please.

Go, dearer than life to thy Caroline's heart,
　The din of the battle's begun ;
Go, share in each danger a valorous part,
　And fight till the victory is won.

The cherub of safety before thee shall fly,
　And shelter the brave with her wing ;

And Mercy shall guard thee when danger is nigh
And thee to my bosom shall bring.

And think not, dear youth, for thy absence I'll moan
Or weep when I bid thee adieu;
I'll twine the bright chaplet to greet thy return,
And live, dearest soldier, for you.

Thy country has call'd thee, the mandate obey,
O ! snatch not another adieu ;
The tear I'll suppress—gallant soldier, away !
I'll live for my country and you.

THE AMERICAN FLAG.

Proud flag of my country ! all gallantly streaming
In the breeze of the battle when glory appears,
The stern scarlet blaze of its hurricane braving,
While mercy hangs round with her olive and tears

Proud flag of my country ! 'tis transport to meet
Some smoke-colored hero, who bled under thee;
As he rushed after victory's blood-dripping feet,
And grasped the wild laurel that blossoms o'er
the sea.

Yes, yes, if there's one whom a nation should love,
One high-minded man, whom e'en angels admire ;
It is he, who with spirit all flushed from above
With the rich loyal bloom of the patriot's fire,

Dares stand between danger and thee, all the hour
When the tyrant would tread on thy peace and thy
   power.
                    Dares stand, &c.

IMMORTAL WASHINGTON.

Columbia's greatest glory
Was her loved chief, fair Freedom's friend;
  Whose fame, renown'd in story,
Shall last till time itself shall end.
    Ye muses bring
    Your harps, and sing
Sweet lays that in smooth numbers run,
  In praise of our loved hero,
The great, the god-like Washington.

His fame, through future ages,
Columbia's free-born sons shall raise,
  The theme each heart engages,
All tongues shall join to sing his praise.
    With joy sound forth
    His virtue's worth,
And tell the glorious acts he's done.
    Of all mankind, the greatest
Was our beloved Washington.

And, O! thou great Creator,
Who form'd his youth, and watch'd his age,
  Since thou, in course of nature,
Hast call'd him from his earthly stage,

Great Power above,
Enthroned in love,
Who was before this world begun,
Receive into thy bosom
Our virtuous hero Washington.

———

LONG LIVE AMERICA.
AIR—"*Gaily the Troubadour.*"

Long live America—
  Home of the Free !
Hopes of the myriad throng
  Centre on thee !
CHORUS.
Long live America,
  Land of the Free ;
" Firmly stand, Freedom's Land,
  Long life to thee !"
" Land where our fathers died,"
  For liberty,
Land where their ashes are—
  Blessings on thee !
            Long live America, &c.

Brightly thy holy light
  Shines through the morn ;
Soon shall its radiance
  All lands adorn !
            Long live America, &c.

As sands on Ocean's shore,
  Freemen abide ;
Scattered thine empire o'er,
  Thickly and wide !
          Long live America, &c.

May Faction ever sleep,
  Peace ever reign ;
Hand-in-hand freemen stand,
  Rights to maintain !
          Long live America, &c.

May streams of Knowledge flow,
  Throughout the land ;
Thus shall the Light of Life
  All minds expand !
          Long live America, &c.

God save America !
  Oh, may she be
O'ershadow'd evermore,
  FATHER, by Thee !
          Long live America, &c.

America ! Bright name !
  In strength and pride,
Blaze thine altar-flame,
  'Tween th' Ocean's tide !
          Long live America, &c.

Bright home of Freedom's shrine,
  May'st thou e'er be

Guided by Power Divine!
Long life to thee!
Long live America, &c.

INDEPENDENCE DAY.

Squeak the fife and beat the drum,
Independence day has come,
Let the roasting pig be bled,
Quick twist off the rooster's head,
Quickly rub the pewter-platter,
Heap the nut-cakes, fried in butter;
Set the cups and beaker-glass,
The pumpkin and the apple-sauce.

Send the keg to shop for brandy;
Maple sugar we have handy.
Independent, staggering Dick,
A noggin mix of swinging thick;
Sal put on your russet skirt,
Jonathan get your boughten shirt,
To-day we dance to tiddle diddle—
There comes Sambo with his fiddle.

Sambo, take a dram of whiskey,
And play us Yankee Doodle friskey.
Moll, come leave your wicked tricks
And let us have a reel of six.
Father and mother shall make two—
Sal, Moll, and I stand all a row;

Sambo, play and dance with quality,
This is the day of blest equality.

Father and mother are but men,
And Sambo—is a citizen—
Come foot it Sal—Moll, figure in,
And mother, you dance up to him.
Now saw as fast as ever you can do,
And father you cross o'er to Sambo—
Thus we dance, and thus we play,
On glorious Independent Day.

Encore Verses.

Rub more rosin on your bow,'
And let us have another go—
Zounds! as sure as eggs and bacon
Here's ensign Sneak, and uncle Deacon,.
Aunt Thiah, and there's Bets behind her,
On blundering mare, than beetle blinder,
And there's the squire, too, with his lady;.
Sal, hold the beast, I'll take the baby.

Moll, bring the squire the great arm-chair,
Good folks we're glad to see you here,—
Jonathan get the great case bottle,
Your teeth can pull its corn-cob stopple.
Ensign—Deacon, never mind,
Squire drink until you're blind—
Thus we drink and dance away,
This glorious Independent Day.

·PAUL JONES.

An American frigate from Baltimore came,
Her guns mounted forty, the Richard by name,
Went to cruise in the channel of old England;
With a noble commander, Paul Jones was the man.

We had not sail'd long before we did espy   .
A large forty-four, and a twenty close by;
Those two warlike ships, full laden with store,
Our captain pursued to the bold Yorkshire shore.

At the hour of twelve, Pierce came along-side,
With a fond speaking trumpet, whence came you?
  he cried,
Quick, give me an answer; I hailed you before,
Or this very instant a broad-side I'll pour.

Paul Jones, he exclaimed, my brave boys, we'll not
 . run,
Let every brave seaman stand close to his gun;
When a broad-side was fired by these brave Eng-
  lishmen,
And we bold Buckskin heroes returned it again.

We fought them five glasses, five glasses most hot,
Till fifty brave seamen lay dead on the spot;
And full seventy more lay bleeding in their gore,
Whilst the Pierce's loud cannon on the Richard did
  roar.
Our gunner affrighted, unto Paul Jones he came,
Our ship is a sinking, likewise in a flame;

Paul Jones he replied, in the height of his pride,
If we can do no better, we'll sink along-side.

At length our shot flew so quick, they could not
    stand,
The flag of proud Britain was forced to come down ;
The Lion bore down and the Richard did rake,
Which caused the heart of brave Richard to ache.

Come now my brave Buckskins, we've taken a prize,
A large forty-four, and a twenty likewise ;
They are both noble vessels, well laden with store !
We will toss off the can to our country once more.

God help the poor widows, who shortly must weep,
For the loss of their husbands now sunk in the deep ;
We'll drink to brave Paul Jones, who with sword in
    hand,
Shone foremost in action, and gave us command.

RED, WHITE AND BLUE.

Oh, Columbia the gem of the ocean,
    The home of the brave and the free,
The shrine of each patriot's devotion,
    A world offers homage to thee.
Thy mandates make heroes assemble,
    When liberty's form stands in view,
Thy banners make tyrants tremble,
    When borne by the red, white and blue.
      When borne by the red, white and blue,

When borne by the red, white and blue,
   Thy banners makes tyrants tremble,
When borne by the red, white and blue.

When war waged its wide desolation,
   And threatened our land to deform,
The ark then of freedom's foundation,
   Columbia rode safe through the storm.
With her garland of victory o'er her,
   When so proudly she bore her bold crew
With her flag proudly floating before her,
   The boast of the red, white and blue.
                The boast of, &c.

The wine cup, the wine cup bring hither,
   And fill you it to the brim,
May the wreath they have won never wither
   Nor the star of their glory grow dim.
May the service united not sever,
   And hold to their colours so true,
The army and the navy forever,
   Three cheers for the red, white and blue.
                Three cheers for, &c.

THE YANKEE VOLUNTEER.

The days of seventy-six, my boys,
   We ever must revere,
Our fathers' took their muskets then,
   To fight for freedom dear.

PATRIOTIC SONGSTER.

Upon the plains of Lexington,
   They 'made the foe look queer,
Oh, 'tis great delight to march and **fight,**
   As a Yankee volunteer,
   (*Spoken.*) Ready ! aim ! fire !

Then next on famous Bunker hill,
   Our standard they did rear ;
'Twas there our gallant Warren fell,
   I tell it with a tear ;
But for their victory that day,
   The foe did pay full dear.
                Oh, 'tis great delight, &c.

Through snow and ice, at Trenton, boys,
   They cross'd the Delaware ;
Led by immortal Washington,
   No danger did they fear.
They gave the foe a drubbing, boys,
   Then back to town did steer.
                Oh, 'tis great delight, &c.

At Saratoga, next, my boys,
   Burgoyne they beat severe ;
And at the seige of Yorktown,
   They gained their cause so dear,
Cornwallis then gave up his sword,
   Whilst Freedom's son's did cheer.
                Oh, 'tis great delight, &c.

Throughout our latest struggle, boys,
   We still victorious were,

And Jackson's deeds, at New-Orleans,
　In bright array appear ;
His virtues and his bravery,
　Each freeman must revere.
　　　　　　　Oh, 'twas his delight, &c.

And now for the little Texas, boys,
　Where freedom is held dear,
From the tyrant—Santa Anna's hands,
　Determined to be clear ;
For Houston was the gallant lad,
　That used him so severe.
　　　　　　　Oh, it's our delight, &c.

And should a foeman e'er again,
　Upon our coast appear,
There's hearts around me brave and true,
　Who'd quickly volunteer,
To drive invaders from the soil,
　Columbia's sons hold dear ;
Oh, they'd each delight to march and fight,
　Like Yankee volunteers.

THE SAILOR'S RETURN.

Poor Bessy was a sailor's wife,
　And he was off to sea !
Her only child was by her side,
　And who as sad as she ?
" Forget me not, forget me not,"

When you are far from me ;
And whatsoe'er poor Bessy's lot,
　She will remember thee !

A twelvemonth scarce had past away,
　As it was told to me ;
When Willy with a gladsome heart,
　Came home again from sea.
He bounded up the craggy path,
　And sought his cottage door ;
But his poor wife and lovely child,
　Poor Willy saw no more !

"Forget me not, forget me not,"
　The words rung in' his ear ;
He asked the neighbors one by one,
　Each answered with a tear !
They pointed to the old church-yard,
　And there his youthful bride ;
With the pretty child he loved so well,
　Were resting side by side !

THE FISHERMAN'S BOY.

Down in the lowlands a poor boy did wander,
　Down in the lowlands a poor boy did roam,
By his friends he was deserted, he looked so dejected,
　Cries the poor little fisherman, so far away from
　　home.

Oh ! where is my cot, oh ! where is my father
　Alas ! they are gone, and caused me to roam,

My mother died on the pillow, my father sunk in
    the billow,
  Cries the poor little fisherman, so far away from
    home.

Bitter was the night, and loud roared the thunder,
  The lightning did flash, and our ship was over-
    thrown,
I clasped my master round O, I gained my native
    ground O,
  Lost my father in the deep, far, far away from
    home.

I waited on the beach, right round me roared the
    water,
  I waited on the beach, but alas! no father came,
It's now I'm forced to range, exposed to every dan-
    ger,
  Cries the poor little fisnerman, so far away from
    home.

A lady when she heard him, she opened her window,
  In the kindest manner desired him to come,.
Tears fell from her eyes as she heard his mournful
    cries,
  Cries the poor little fisherman, so far away from
    home.

She begged of her father to find him some employ
    ment,
  She begged of her father, no more to let him roam,
Her father said, don't grieve me, this boy shall nev-
    er leave me,

Poor boy I will relieve thee, so far away from
home.

Many years he labored to serve his noble master,
Many years he labored, till a man he became,
It's now I'll tell each stranger, the hardships and
the danger,
Of a poor little fisherman's boy, far, far away
from home.

FISHERMAN'S GIRL.

It was down in the country, a poor girl was weeping,
It was down in the country, poor Mary Ann did
mourn,
She belongs to this nation, I have lost each dear re-
lation,
Cries a poor little fisherman's girl—my friends are
dead and gone.

Oh, who has a soft heart to give me some shelter,
For the bitter winds do blow, and dreadful is the
storm,
I have no father nor mother, but I've a tender
brother,
Cries the poor little fisherman's girl—my friends
are dead and gone.

Oh, once I'd enjoyment, my friends they reared me
tender,
I pass'd with my brother each happy night and
morn,

But death has made a slaughter, poor father's in the
    water,
    Cries a poor little fisherman's girl—my friends are
    dead and gone.

So fast falls the snow, and I cannot find shelter,
    So fast falls the snow, and I must hasten to the
    thorn,
For my covering is the bushes, my bed is the rushes,
    Cried the poor little fisherman's girl—my friends
    are dead and gone.

It happened as she passed by a very noble cottage,
    A gentleman, he heard her his breast for her did
    burn,
Crying, come in poor lonely creature! he viewed
    each drooping feature,
    Of a poor little fisherman's girl—whose friends
    are dead and gone.

He took her to the fire, and when he'd warm'd and
    fed her,
    The tears began to fall, he fell on her breast for-
    lorn,
Crying, live with me forever, we part again no,
    never,
    You are my dearest sister! our friends are dead
    and gone.

So now she's got a home, she's living with her
    brother,
    So now she's got a home, and the needy ne'er does
    scorn,

For God was her protector, likewise her kind conductor,
  The poor little fisherman's girl—when her friends
  were dead and gone.

———

THE MARINER'S GRAVE.

I remember the night was stormy and wet,
  And dismally dash'd the dark wave,
    While the rain and the sleet,
    Cold and heavily beat
On the Mariner's new dug grave.

I remember 'twas down in a darksome dale,
  And near to a dreary cave,
    Where the wild winds wail,
    Round the wanderer pale,
That I saw the Mariner's grave.

I remember how slowly the bearers trod,
  And how sad was the look they gave,
    As they rested their load,
    Near its last abode,
And gazed on the Mariner's grave.

I remember no sound did the silence break,
  As the corpse to the earth they gave,
    Save the night-bird's shriek,
    And the coffin's creak
As it sunk in the Mariner's grave.

I remember a tear that slowly slid
  Down the cheek of a messmate brave,
      It fell on the lid
      And soon was hid,
  For closed was the Mariner's grave.

Now o'er his lone bed the briar creeps,
  And the wild flow'rs mournfully wave
      And the willow weeps,
      And the moon-beam sleeps,
  On the Mariner's silent grave.

A WET SHEET AND A FLOWING SEA.

A wet sheet! and a flowing sea,
  And a wind that follows fast,
And fills the white and rustling sail,
  And bends the gallant mast;
And bends the gallant mast, my boys!
  While like an eagle free,
Away our good ship flies, and leaves
  Columbia to our lee.
            CHORUS.
  Oh, give me a wet sheet, and a flowing sea
    And a wind that follows fast,
  And fills the white and rustling sail,
    And bends the gallant mast.

For a soft and gentle wind,
  I heard a fair one cry,

But give to me the roaring breeze,
 And white waves heaving high ;
And white waves heaving high, my boys !
 The good ship tight and free ;
The world of waters is our home,
 And merry men are we.   Oh, give, &c

There's tempest in yon horned moon,
 And lightning in yon cloud—
And hark, the music, mariners,
 The wind is piping loud,
The wind is piping loud, my boys !
 The lightning flashes free ;
While the hollow oak our palace is,
 Our heritage the sea !   Oh, give, &c.

THE MINUTE GUN AT SEA.

Let him who sighs in sadness here,
Rejoice, and know a friend is near ;
What heavenly sounds are those I hear ?
What being comes the gloom to cheer ?
When in the storm on Albion's coast,
The night-watch guards his weary post,
 From thoughts of danger free ;
He marks some vessels dusky form,
And hears amid the howling storm,
 The minute gun at sea.

Swift on the shore a hardy few,

The life-boat man'd with a gallant crew,
  And dare the dang'rous wave ;
Through the wild surf, they cleave their way,
Lost in the foam nor know dismay,
  For they go the crew to save.
But, oh, what raptures fill each breast,
Of the hapless crew of the ship distressed !
Then, landed safe, what joys to tell,
Of all the dangers that befel.
Then is heard no more,
By the watch on shore,
  The minute gun at sea.

THE RETIRED SOLDIER.

The retired soldier, bold and brave,
  Now rests his weary feet,
And in the shelter of the grave,
  Has found a safe retreat.
To him the trumpet's piercing breath,
  To arms, they call in vain ;
For quartered in the arms of death,
  He'll never, never march again.
CHORUS.
March, march again, march, march again,
March, march again, march, march again,
For quartered in the arms of death,
He'll never, never march again.

A day when he left his father's home

The charms of war to try,
O'er regions hath he had to roam,
No friend or mother nigh.
But still he marched contented on,
Met danger, death and pain,
And now at rest, all dangers o'er,
He'll never, never march again.

March, march, &c.

The sweets of spring by beauteous hand,
Lay scattered on his bier,
Whilst listening round his comrades stand,
Gave honest Ned a tear.
Whilst lovely Kate, for Ned's delight,
Chief mourner of the train,
Cried, as she view'd the solemn sight,
He'll never, never march again.

March, march, &c.

THE GHOST OF POLLY ROCK AND HER TWO BANTLINGS.

When I was but a tiny boy,
And sailed on board a privateer,
Three dreadful ghosts did me annoy,
And to my sight did oft appear!
A woman tall, who, on each arm,
A little pale-faced bantling bore,
And cried, 'O! we'll do no harm,
For we, alas! are no more!'

'The captain of your ship,' she cried,
  'My love and truth did sore betray;
And these poor babes with me have died,
  Who might have lived another day!'
'Dear ghost,' I said, 'all this is hard,
  If Captain Rock be such an elf,
While I am watching on my guard,
  I think you'd better tell himself.'

She took the hint—down slid the ghost
  To where the Captain slept below;
She drew the curtains to the posts,
  And pale she gazed as drifted snow!
'I'm come,' she cried, 'bold Captain Rock,
  To plague thy heart our ghosts are come,
Full cold I am as marble block,
  And eke the young ones, Sal and Tom.'

'Dear Polly Rock,' the Captain said,
  And trembled much as he thus spoke;
'I never heard that you were dead,
  And fear, my love, that you but joke.'
To prove her truth they vanished straight,
  And at their heels a fiery flame;
The Captain roared out for his mate,
  Drank off his grog—and slept again.

HULL'S VICTORY.

A proud stately figure from Britania there came,
With a haughty commander, James Dacres by name.
He toss'd and he swaggered upon the high seas,
So sure was he of taking each vessel with ease.

But another proud frigate there ploughed through
    the waves,
With these words at her mast head, we are no Brit-
    ish slaves,
We've a noble commander, his name's Isaac Hull,
Who, with the good Constitution, is a match for
    John Bull.

The British they spy'd us, and on us bore down,
And thought soon to make us subject to the crown:
"Huzza now," cries Dacres, "we'll take her with
    ease,"
"Stop a bit," says our captain, "not so fast, if you
    please."

The British bore down with a hot raking fire,
Dacres stood on the quarter, a breathing his ire;
Hull opened our ports, and we showed them such
    play,
Which soon carried our mizzen and fore-mast away.

We ran along-side, giving three hearty cheers,
Which rang like a knell in these bold Britons' ears;
"Huzza, now," cries Hull, "boys, we'll at them
    again,

And we'll lay this proud Guerriere, a wreck on the
main.

We rammed well our guns, to make each shot tell,
When at our next broadside, her main-mast it fell,
And with it came ensign, rigging and all ;
Success to our good Yankee powder and ball.

Now we'll drink to brave Hull, and the bold
   Yankee tars,
Who fought 'neath the banner of the broad stripes
   and stars,
We'll pass round the can, boys, and each drink our
   fill,
Not forgetting the glories of old Bunker Hill.

WHERE'S MY SOLDIER LOVER.

Where, where's my soldier lover ?—
   Where, 'mid the dead or few
That fight, though hope is over ?—
   Warrior, answer true.
I twined him, when he left me,
   A scarf, around his spear ;—
Oh ! has my gift bereft me
   Of all I held most dear ?

Say, have they mark'd him for it ?
   Was it through that he fell ?—
But still I'm glad he wore it—
   It suited freedom well ;

Of blue and green I made it,
　Colors that nature loves ;
With blue the sky is shaded,
　With green the vales and groves.

There is a warhorse flying
　Across the battle plain—
Where is the soldier lying?
　Is he amid the slain ?
Oh ! let me to the slaughter—
　It may be vain to try ;
But is not Poland's daughter
　Fit with her sons to die ?
　Where, where's my soldier lover, &c.

———

SOLDIER'S DREAM.

Our bugles sang truce, for the night cloud had
　low'rd,
And the sentinel stars set their watch in the sky ;
And thousands had sunk on the ground overpow'rd,
　The weary to sleep, and the wounded to die.

When reposing that night on my pallet of straw,
　By the wolf-scaring faggot that guarded the slain ;
At the dead of the night a sweet vision I saw,
　And thrice e'er the morning, I dreamt it again.

Methought from the battle-field's dreadful array,
　Far I had roamed on a desolate track ;
'Twas autumn—and sunshine arose on the way,

To the home of my father that welcom'd me
back.

I flew to the pleasant fields traversed so oft,
   In life's morning march when my bosom was
   young,
I heard my own mountain-goats bleating aloft,
   And knew the sweet strain that the corn-reapers
   sung.

Then pledg'd we the wine cup, and fondly I swore,
   From my home, and my weeping friends never to
   part;
My little ones kiss'd me a thousand times o'er
   And my wife sobb'd aloud in the fulness of heart.

Stay, stay with us—rest, thou art weary and worn,
   And fain was the war-broken soldier to stay;
But sorrow returned with dawning of morn,
   And the voice of my dreaming ere melted away

BILLY TAYLOR.

Billy Taylor was a brisk young fellow,
   Full of fun and full of glee,
Hnd his mind he did discover,
   To a lady fair and free.

Four and twenty brisk young fellows,
   Dress'd they were in rich array;
And they took poor Billy Taylor,

Whom they press'd and sent to sea.

Then his true love follow'd after,
　Under the name of Richard Carr;
Her lilly hands were soon daub'd over,
　With the filthy pitch and tar.

Now behold the first engagement,
　Boldly she fights among the rest,
The wind it blew her jacket open,
　And discovered her milk-white breast.

When the captain smiling viewed it,
　Said, " what wind has blown you here?"
" Sir, I'm come to seek my true love,
　Whom you press'd, and I love dear."

' If you've come to see your true love,
　Tell me his uame I pray;'
' Sir, his name is Billy Taylor,
　Whom you press'd and sent to sea.'

' If his name is Billy Taylor,
　He is both cruel and severe;
For rise up early in the morning,
　And you'll see him with his lady fair.'

With that she rose up next mornin
　Early by the break of day;
And there she saw Billy Taylor,
　Dancing with his lady gay.

She then called for a sword and pistol,

Which were brought at her command,
And quickly shot bold Billy Taylor,
With his true love in his hand.

When the captain came to know it,
    He much applauded what she had done;
And immediately made her first lieutenant,
    Of the glorious Thunder Bomb.

———

WILLIAM TELL.

When William Tell was doom'd to die,
    Or hit the mark upon his infant's head—
The bell toll'd out, the hour was nigh,
    And soldiers march'd with grief and dread
The warrior came, serene and mild,
    Gazed all around with dauntless look,
Till his fond boy unconscious smiled;
    Then nature and the father spoke,
And now each gallant Swiss his grief partakes,
            For they sigh,
            And wildly cry,
Poor William Tell, once hero of the Lakes,

And soon is heard the muffled drum,
    And straight the pointed arrow flies;
The trembling boy expects his doom,
    All, all shriek out—" he dies! he dies!"
When lo! the lofty trumpet sounds!
    The mark is hit! the child is free!

Into his father's arms he bounds,
  Inspired by love and liberty.

And now each gallant Swiss their joy partakes,
    For mountains ring,
    Whilst they sing,
Live, William Tell, the hero of the Lakes.

THE GALLANT HUSSAR.

A damsel possessed of great beauty,
  She stood by her own father's gate,
The gallant Hussars were on duty,
  To view them this maiden did wait.
Their horses were capering and prancing,
  Their accoutrements shone like a star,
From the plains they were nearer advancing,
  She espied her young gallant Hussar.

Their pellisses were slung o'er their shoulders
  So careless they seem'd for to ride ;
So warlike appeared those young soldiers,
  With glittering swords by their sides ;
To the barracks next morning so early,
  This damsel she went in her car,
Because that she loved him sincerely—
  Young Edward, the gallant Hussar.

It was there she conversed with her soldier,
  These words they were heard for to say—
Said Jane, " I've a heart none more bolder,

For to follow my laddy awa."
" Oh, fie !" said young Edward, "be steady
And think of the dangers of war,
When the trumpet sounds I must be ready,
So wed not your gallant Hussar."

" For twelve months on bread and cold water,
My parents confined me for you,
Oh, hard-hearted friends to their daughter,
Whose heart it is loyal and true,
Unless they confine me forever,
Or banish me from you afar,
I will follow my soldier forever,
To wed with my gallant Hussar.

Said Edward, "your friends you must mind them,
Or else you are forever undone,
They will leave you no portion behind them,
So pray do my company shun."
She said, "if you will be true hearted,
I have gold of my uncle's in store,
From this time no more we'll be parted,
I will wed with my gallant Hussar."

As he gazed on each beautiful feature,
The tears they did fall from each eye,
"I will wed with this beautiful creature,
To forsake cruel war," he did cry.
So now they're united together,
Friends think of them now they're afar,
Crying, " heaven bless them now and forever,
Young Jane and her gallant Hussar."

THE SEAMAN'S HOME.

O you, whose lives on land are pass'd,
  And keep from dangerous seas aloof;
Who careless listen to the blast,
  Or beating rains upon the roof;
You little heed how seamen fare—
Condemn'd the angry storm to bear.

Sometimes while breakers vex the tide,
  He takes his station on the deck;
And now, lash'd o'er the vessel's side,
  He clears away the cumbring wreck;
Yet, while the billows o'er him foam,
The ocean is his only home!

Still fresher blows the midnight gale!
  "All hands reef top-sails," are the cries,
And, while the clouds the heavens veil,
  Aloft to reef the sails he flies.

A SOLDIER TO-NIGHT IS OUR GUEST.

Fan, fan the gay hearth, and fling back the barr'd
    door,
Strew, strew the fresh rushes around on the floor,
And blithe be the welcome in every breast,
For a soldier—a soldier to-night is our guest.

All honor to him, who, when danger afar
Had lighted for ruin his ominous star,

Left pleasures and country, and kindred behind,
And sped to the shock on the wings of the wind.

If you value the blessings that shine at our hearth—
The wife's smiling welcome, the infant's sweet mirth—
While they chrrm us at eve, let us think upon those
Who have bought with their blood, our domestic
    repose.

Then share with a soldier your hearth and your home,
And warm be your greeting whene'er he shall come;
Let love light a welcome in every breast,
For a soldier—a soldier to-night is our guest.

THE LAND OF THE WEST.

Oh, come to the West love—oh, come there with
    me ;
'Tis a sweet land of verdure that springs from the
    sea,
Where fair Plenty smiles from her Emerald throne ;
Oh, come to the West, and I'll make thee my own !
I'll guard thee, I'll tend thee, I'll love thee the best,
And you'll say there's no land like the land of the
    West !

The South has its roses and bright skies of blue,
But ours are more sweet with love's own changeful
    hue—
Half sunshine, half tears—like the girl I love best;

Oh, what is the South to the beautiful West ?
Then come to the West, and the rose on thy mouth
Will be sweeter to me than the flow'rs of the South !

The North has its snow-tow'rs of dazzling array,
All sparkling with gems in the ne'er-setting day ;
There the Storm-king may dwell in the halls he
    loves best,
But the soft-breathing Zephyr he plays in the West.
Then come there with me, where no cold wind doth
    blow,
And thy neck will seem fairer to me than the snow !

The Sun, in the gorgeous East, chaseth the night
When he riseth, refresh'd, in his glory and might ;
But where does he go when he seeks his sweet rest ?
Oh, doth he not haste to the beautiful West ?
Then come there with me, 'tis the land I love best,
'Tis the land of my sires!—'tis my own darling
    West !

        ————

THE AMERICAN GIRL.

Our hearts are with our native land,
  Our song is for her glory ;
Her warrior's wreath is in our hand
  Our lips breathe out her story.
Her lofty hills and valleys green,
  Are shining bright before us ;
And like a rainbow sign is seen
  Her proud flag waving o'er us.

And there are smiles upon our lips
　For those who meet her foemen,
For glory's star knows no eclipse,
　When smiled upon by women.
For those who brave the mighty deep,
　And scorn the threat of danger,
We've smiles to cheer—and tears to weep
　For every ocean ranger.

Our hearts are with our native land,
　Our songs are for her freedom ;
Our prayers are for the gallant band
　Who strike where honor leads them
We love the taintless air we breathe,
　'Tis freedom's endless power,
We'll twine for him an endless wreath
　Who scorns a tyrant's power.

They tell of France's beauties fair,
　Of Italy's proud daughters ;
Of Scotland's lasses—England's fair,
　And nymphs of Shannon's waters.
We need not boast their haughty charms,
　Though lords around them hover,
Our glory lies in freedom's arms,
　A Freeman for a lover.

THE BATTLE OF BALTIMORE.

Old Ross, Cockburn, and Cochran too,
　And many a bloody villian more,

Swore with their bloody savage crew,
    That they would plunder Baltimore.
But General Winder being afraid
    That his militia would not stand,
He sent away to crave the aid
    Of a few true Virginians.
        Then up we rose with hearts elate,
        To help our suffering sister state, &c.

When first our orders we received,
    For to prepare without delay,
Our wives and sweethearts for to leave,
    And to the army march away.
Although it griev'd our hearts full sore,
    To leave our sweet Virginia shore,
We kiss'd our sweethearts o'er and o'er,
    And marched like true Virginians.
        Adieu awhile, sweet girls adieu,
        With honor we'll return to you.

With rapid marches on we went,
    To leave our sweet Virginia shore,
No halt was made, no time was spent,
    Till we arrived at Baltimore.
The Baltimoreans did us greet,
    The ladies clapt their lily white hands,
Exclaiming as we passed the street,
    Welcome ye brave Virginians.
        May heaven all your foes confound,
        And send you home with laurels crown'd.

We had not been in quarters long,
　　Before we heard the dread alarms.
The cannon roared the bells did ring,
　　The drum did beat to arms, to arms.
Then up we rose to face our foes,
　　Determined to meet them on the strand,
And drive them back from fair freedom's shore,
　　Or die like brave Virginians.
　　　In heaven above we placed our trust,
　　　Well knowing that our cause was just.

Then Ross he landed at North Point,
　　With seven thousand men or more,
And swore by that time next night,
　　That he would be in Baltimore.
But Striker met him on the strand,
　　Attended by a chosen band,
Where he received a fatal shot,
　　From a brave Pennsylvanian—
　　　Whom heaven directed to the field,
　　　To make his haughty Briton yield, &c

Then Cockburn he drew up his fleet,
　　To bombard Fort McHenry,
A thinking that our men, of course,
　　Would take afright and run away.
The fort was commanded by a patriot band,
　　As ever grac'd fair freedom's land,
As he who did the fort command,
　　Was a true blue Virginian.
　　　Long may we have brave Armstead's name

Recorded on the book of fame, &c.

A day and a night they tried their might,
    But found their bombs did not prevail,
And seeing their army put to flight,
    They weighed anchor and made sail.
Resolving to return again,
    To execute their former plan ;
But if they do they'll find us still,
    That we are brave Viaginians.
      And they shall know before they've **done**
      That they are not in Washington.

But now their shipping's out of sight,
    And each man take a parting glass,
Drink to his true love and heart's de**light,**
    His only joy and bosom friend,
For I might as well drink a health,
    For I hate to see good liquor stand,
That America may always boast,
    That we are brave Virginians.

BATTLE OF BUNKER HILL.

It was on the seventeenth, by break **of day,**
    The Yankees did surprise us,
With their strong works they had thrown **up,**
    To burn the town and drive us.

But soon we had an order come,
    An order to defeat them ;

Like rebels stout, they stood it out,
  And thought we ne'er could beat them.

About the hour of twelve that day,
  An order came for marching,
With three good flints, and sixty rounds,
  Each man hoped to discharge them.

We marched down to the Long Wharf,
  Where boats were ready waiting;
With expedition we embark'd,
  Our ships kept cannonading.

And when our boats all filled were
  With officers and soldiers,
With as good troops as England had,
  To oppose who dare control us?

Aud when our boats all filled were,
  We row'd in line of battle,
Where showers of ball like hail did fly,
  Our cannon loud did rattle.

There Copp's Hill battery, near Charlestowr
  Our twenty-fours they played;
And the three frigates in the stream,   .
  They very well behaved.

The Glasgow frigate clear'd the shore,
  All at the time of landing,
With her grape-shot and cannon-balls,
  No Yankee e'er could stand them.

And when we landed on the shore,
  We draw'd up all together;
The Yankees they all mann'd their works,
  And thought we'd ne'er come hither.

But soon they did perceive brave Howe,
  Brave Howe, our bold commander;
With granadiers, and infantry,
  We made them to surrender.

Brave William Howe on our right wing,
  Cried, "Boys, fight on like thunder;
You soon will see the rebels flee,
  With great amaze and wonder."

Now some lay bleeding on the ground,
  And some fell fast a running
O'er hills and dales, and mountains high,
  Crying, "Zounds! brave Howe's a coming."

Brave Howe is so considerate,
  As to guard against all dangers:
He allow'd each half a gill a day,
  To rum we were no strangers.

They began to play on our left wing,
  Where Pigot, he commanded;
But we returned it back again,
  With courage most undaunted.

To our grape-shot and musket-balls,
  To which they were but strangers,
They sought to come with sword in hand,
  But soon they found their danger.

And when their works were got into,
   And put them to the flight, sir,
They pepper'd us, poor British elves,
   And show'd us they could fight, sir.

And when their works we got into,
   With some hard knocks and danger;
Their works we found both firm and strong,
   Too strong for British Rangers.

But as for our artillery,
   They gave all way and run,
For while their ammunition held,
   They gave us Yankee fun.

But our commander, he got broke
   For his misconduct, sure, sir;
The shot he sent for twelve-pound guns,
   Were made for twenty-fours, sir.

There's some in Boston pleased to say,
   As we the field were taking,
We went to kill their countrymen,
   While they their hay were making.

For such stout wings I never saw,
   To hang them all I'd rather;
By making hay with musket-balls,
   Lord Howe, cursedly did bother.

Bad luck to him by land and sea,
   For he's despised by many;

The name of Bunker Hill he dreads,
  Where he was flogg'd most plainly.

And now my song is at an end:
  And to conclude my ditty,
'Tis only Britons ignorant,
  That I most sincerely pity.

As for our king and William Howe,
  And General Gage, if they're taken,
The Yankee will hang their heads up high,
  On that fire hill, call'd Beacon.

THE YANKEE GIRLS.

For England's daughters rosy cheek'd,
  Nor Scotia's lasses fair;
Nor Erin's blooming maiden can
  With the Yankee girls compare;
Though what they tell us of their charms
  All very true may be,
They'll not compare with Yankee girls,
  The Yankee girls for me.

Let Byron of Italian maids,
  In glowing numbers sing,
And let the Turk his Georgian bride,
  And black-eyed Houries bring;
Yet what they tell us of their charms,
  All very true may be,

They'll not compare with Yankee **girls,**
   The Yankee girls for me.

Their faultless forms! their peerless **eyes,**
   As bright as morning dew,
Their cheeks so fair! their spirits light!
   Their hearts so warm and true!
They're chaste as fair, their minds **unchain'd,**
   In thought and action free,
There's nothing like the Yankee **girls,**
   The Yankee girls for me.

Unto Columbia's daughter then,
   We'll drain the goblet dry,
Naught can the universe **produce,**
   With Yankee girls to vie;
O! they're the fairest of the **fair,**
   And ever may they be,
There's nothing like the Yankee **girls,**
   The Yankee girls for me.

THE HUNTERS OF KENTUCKY.

Ye gentlemen and ladies fair,
   Who grace this famous city,
Just listen, if you've time to **spare,**
   While I rehearse a ditty;
And for the opportunity
   Conceive yourselves quite **lucky,**
For 'tis not often that you see

A hunter from Kentucky.
Oh, Kentucky! the hunters of Kentucky.

We are a hardy free-born race,
　　Each man to fear a stranger ;
Whate'er the game we join in chase,
　　Despising toil and danger ;
And if a daring foe annoys,
　　Whate'er his strength and forces,
We'll show him that Kentucky boys
　　Are alligator horses.

　　　　　　　　　Oh, Kentucky ! &c.

ı 'spose you've read it in the prints,
　　How Peckenham attempted
To make old Hickory Jackson wince—
　　But soon his schemes repented;
For we with rifles ready cocked
　　Thought such occasion lucky,
And soon around the general flocked
　　The hunters of Kentucky.

　　　　　　　　　Oh, Kentucky ! &c.

You've heard, I s'pose, how New-Orleans
　　Is famed for wealth and beauty—
There's girls of every hue, it seems,
　　From snowy white, to sooty ;
So Packenham he made his brags,
　　If he in fight was lucky,
He'd have their girls and cotton bags

In spite of old Kentucky.

　　　　　　　Oh, Kentucky ! &c

But Jackson he was wide awake,
　　And wasn't scared at trifles,
For well he knew what aim we take
　　With our Kentucky rifles ;
So he led us down to Cyprus swamp—
　　The ground was low and mucky,
There stood John Bull in martial pomp,
　　And here was old Kentucky.

　　　　　　　Oh, Kentucky ! &c.

A bank was raised to hide our breast
　　Not that we thought of dying,
But then we always like to rest
　　Unless the game is flying ;
Behind it stood our little force—
　　None wished it to be greater,
And every man was half a horse
　　And half an alligator.

　　　　　　　Oh, Kentucky ! &c.

They did not let our patience tire,
　　Before they showed their faces—
We did not choose to waste our fire,
　　So snugly kept our places ;
But when so near to see them wink,
　　We thought it time to stop 'em ;
And 'twould have done you good, I think

To see Kentuckians drop 'em.

Oh, Kentucky! &c.

They found at last 'twas vain to fight,
Where lead was all their booty ;
And so they wisely took to flight,
And left us all our beauty.
And now if danger e'er annoys,
Remember what our trade is ;
Just send for us Kentucky boys,
And we'll protect you ladies.

HURRAH FOR THE WHITE, RED AND BLUE.

Hush'd is the clamorous trumpet of war,
Hush'd, hush'd is the trumpet of war ;
The soldier's retired from the clangour of arms,
The drum rolls a peaceful hurrah.
'Tis cheering to think on the past,
'Tis cheering to think we've been true,
'Tis cheering to look on our stars and our stripes,
And gaze on our white, red and blue.
Hurrah for the white, red and blue,
Hurrah for the white, red and blue,
'Tis cheering to look on our stars and our stripes,
And gaze on our white, red and blue.

Here's a sigh for the brave that are dead,
Here's a sigh for the brave that are dead,
And who would not sigh for the glorious brave,

That rest on a patriot bed ?
'Tis glory, for country to die,
'Ts glory that's solid and true ;
'Tis glory to sleep 'neath our stars and our stripes
And die for our white, red and blue.
Hurrah for the white, red and blue,
Hurrah for the white, red and blue,
'Tis glory to sleep 'neath our stars and our stripes
And die for the white, red, and blue.

Here's freedom of thought and of deed,
Here's freedom in valley and plain,
The first song of freedom that rose on our hills,
Our sea-shore re-echoed again.
'Tis good to love country and friends,
'Tis good to be honest and true ;
'Tis good to die shouting on sea, or on shore
" Hurrah for the white, red, and, blue,"
Hurrah for the white, red, and blue,
Hurrah for the white, red, and blue,
'Tis good to die shouting, at sea or on shore,
" Hurrah for the white, red, and blue !"

THE STAR-SPANGLED BANNER.

O say, can you see by the dawn's early light,
What so proudly we hailed at the twilight's last
gleaming,
Whose broad stripes and bright stars through the
perilous fight,

O'er tho ramparts we watched, were so gallantly
     streaming;
And the rockets red glare, the bombs bursting in air,
Gave proof through the night that our flag was still
     there—
O! say does that star-spangled banner yet wave,
O'er the land of the free and the home of the brave?

On the shore, dimly seen through the mist of the
     deep,
  Where the foe's haughty host in dread silence re-
     poses,
What is that which the breeze o'er the towering
     steep,
  As it fitfully blows, half conceals, half discloses?
Now it catches the gleam of the morning's first
     beam,
In full glory reflected now shines on the stream—
'Tis the star-spangled banner, O! long may it wave
O'er the land of the free, and the home of the brave.

And where is that band which so vauntingly swore,
  That the havoc of war and the battle's confusion,
A home and a country should leave us no more?
  Their blood has washed out their foul footsteps
     pollution,
No refuge could save the hireling and slave
From the terror of flight or the gloom of the grave.
And the star-spangled banner in triumph doth wave
O'er the land of the free and the home of the brave.

O! thus be it ever when freedom shall stand,
  Between their loved home, and the war's desola-
      tion
Blest with victory and peace, may the heaven-res-
      cued land
  Praise the power that hath made and preserved
      us a nation,
Then conquer we must, when our cause it is just,
And this be our motto—In God is our trust!
And the star-spangled banner in triumph shall wave,
O'er the land of the free, and the home of the brave.

HAIL COLUMBIA.

Hail Columbia! happy land!
Hail, ye heroes! heaven-born band!
  Who fought and bled in freedom's cause,
  Who fought and bled in freedom's cause,
And when the storm of war was gone,
Enjoy'd the peace your valor won.
  Let independence be our boast,
  Ever mindful what it cost ;
  Ever grateful for the prize,
  Let its altar reach the skies.
        Firm—united—let us be,
        Rallying round our Liberty;
        As a band of brothers joined
        Peace and safety we shall find.

Immortal patriots! rise once more ;

Defend your rights, defend your shore
  Let no rude foe, with impious hand,
  Let no rude foe, with impious hand,
Invade the shrine where sacred lies
Of toil and blood the well-earned prize.
  While offering peace sincere and just,
  In Heaven we place a manly trust,
  That truth and justice will prevail,
  And every scheme of bondage fail.
      Firm—united, &c.

Sound, sound, the trump of Fame!
Let Washington's great name
  Ring through the world with loud applause,
  Ring through the world with loud applause;
Let every clime to Freedom dear,
Listen with a joyful ear.
  With equal skill, and godlike power,
  Of horrid war; or guides, with ease,
  The happiest times of honest peace.
      Firm—united, &c.

Behold the chief who now commands,
Once more to serve his country, stand—
  The rock on which the storm will beat,
  The rock on which the storm will beat;
But, arm'd in virtue firm and true,
His hopes are fixed on Heaven and you.
  When hope was sinking in dismay,
  And glooms obscured Columbia's day,
  His steady mind, from changes free,

Resolved on death or liberty.
Firm—united, &c.

THE BATTLE OF NEW ORLEANS.

Hail to the hero, the pride of his country,
  Honor'd by all be his ever great name;
Where is the man who presumes with effrontery
  To tarnish the laurels that bloom with his **fame;**
      Down where the waters flow,
      He met the invading foe,
Where great Mississippi resounds with his **fame,**
      There, with his gallant band,
      Nobly sustain'd the land,
And cover'd the foe with confusion and shame.

Loudly the thunders of battle were roaring,
  Hurling defeat in the ranks of the foe,
Proudly above, the proud eagle was soaring,
  The warriors of Britain were prostrate **and low.**
      There with undaunted mein,
      Jackson shone amid the scene;
The red glare of battle, the hero display'd;
      He every bosom fired,
      His voice, every one inspired;
To conquest, to glory, they rush'd undismayed.

Mid volumes of smoke, that the combat enshrouded
  Thy banner, O Freedom! with brilliancy shone,
But Britian, the sun of thy glory was clouded,
  Thy legions were routed, thy hosts overthrown;

No more along the coast,
Is heard their haughty boast,
While beauty and booty the battle impel;
Long they'll lament the day,
When in the mortal fray,
Their hopes were all crush'd with the thousands
who fell.

Hail, thou firm patriot, beloved by the nation,
Thy honor unsoil'd, by integrity tried,
Worthy to fill the most exalted station,
With valor to save, and with skill to preside.
In vain the intriguing foe
Aims the insidious blow,
To blight thy fair laurels, to sully thy fame,
Truth, with the rays of light,
Thy virtues, brave chief, will write,
In the annals of greatness emblazon thy name.

PERRY'S VICTORY.

Ye tars of Columbia, give ear to my story,
Who fought with the brave Perry, where cannon
did roar ;
Your valor has gain'd you an immortal glory,
A fame that shall last till time is no more.
Columbian tars are the true sons of Mars,
They rake fore and aft, when they fight on the
deep ;
On the bed of Lake Erie, commanded by Perry,

They caused many Britons to take their last sleep.

The tenth of September, let us all remember,
   So long as the globe on her axis rolls round ;
Our tars and marines, on Lake Erie were seen,
   To make the proud flag of Great Britain come
      down.
Her guns they did roar with such terrific power,
   That savages trembled at the dreadful sound.

The Lawrence sustained a most dreadful fire ;
   She fought three to one, for two glasses or more ;
While Perry, undaunted, did firmly stand by her,
   The proud foe on her heavy broadside did pour :
Her masts being shatter'd, her rigging all tatter'd,
   Her booms and her yards being all shot away ;
And few left on deck to manage the wreck,
   Our hero on board her no longer could stay.

In this situation, the pride of our nation,
   Sure Heaven had guarded unhurt all the while,
While many a hero, maintaining his station,
   Fell close by his side, and was thrown on the pile.
But mark you, and wonder, when elements thunder,
   When death and destruction are stalking all
      round,
His flag he did carry on board the Niagara ;
   Such valor on record was never yet found.

There is one gallant act of our noble commander,
   While writing my song, I must notice with pride ;

While launch'd in the boat, that carried the
    standard,
  A ball whistled through her, just close by his side,
Says Perry, " The rascals intend for to drown us,
  But push on, my brave boys, you never need fear !"
And with his own coat he plugg'd up the boat,
  And through fire and sulphur away he did steer.

The famed Niagara, now proud of her Perry,
  Display'd all her banners in gallant array ;
And twenty-five guns on her deck she did carry,
  Which soon put an end to this bloody affray.
The rear of our fleet was brought up complete,
  The signal was given to break through the line ;
While starboard and larboard, and from every quar
    ter,
  The lamps of Columbia did gloriously shine.

The bold British Lion roared out his last thunder,
  When Perry attacked him close in the rear ;
Columbia's eagle soon made him crouch under,
  And roar out for quarter, as soon you shall hear
O, had you been there, I now do declare,
  Such a sight as you never had seen before,
Six red blody flags, that no longer could wag,
  All lay at the feet of our brave commodore.

Brave Elliot, whose valor must now be recorded,
  On board the Niagara so well play'd his part,
His gallant assistance to Perry afforded,

We'll place him in the second on Lake Erie's
    chart.
In the midst of the battle, when guns they did rattle,
    The Lawrence a wreck, and the men 'most all
        slain ;
Away he did steer, and brought up the rear,
    And by this manœuvre the victory was gain'd.

May heaven still smile on the shades of our heroes,
    Who fought in the conflict, their country to save,
And check the proud spirit of those murdering
       bravoes,
    That wish to divide us and make us all slaves.
Columbians sing, and make the woods ring,
    We'll toast those brave heroes by sea and by land ;
While Britons drink cherry, Columbians, Perry,
    We'll toast him about with full glass in hand.

THE END.

THE STARS AND STRIPES SONGSTER.

CONTENTS :

Copies mailed to any address, free of postage, upon receipt of Ten Cents.

BRYANT'S POWER OF MUSIC.

CONTENTS :

[Turn Over.]

Copies mailed to any address, free of postage, upon receipt of Ten Cents.

THE TEDDY REGAN SONGSTER.

CONTENTS:

BRYANT'S SONGS FROM DIXIE'S LAND.

CONTENTS:

A Dollar or Two.
Annie Laurie.
Annie Lisle.
Annie, We have Parted.
Ben Bolt.
Billy Barlow,
Brave Old Oak.
Bully for All.
Clap your Hands.
Cruelty to Johnny.
Days of Absence.
Deal with Me Kindly.
Dearest Spot on Eearth.
Dixie's Land, No. 1.
    "   " No. 2.
    "   " No. 3.
Down in the Dell
Down the River.
Dream of Bonaparte.
Ever of Thee.
Far o'er the Deep Blue Sea.
Gipsey Davy.
Going Around the Horn.
Grave of Bonaparte.
Gum-Tree Canoe.
Have you Seen My Sister?
Hark! I hear an Angel Sing.
Happy Land of Canaan.
Home Again.
I'm Going to Dixie.
Joe Bowers.
Life let us Cherish.
Lord Lovel.
Loving Hearts at Home.

Maggie, the Pride of the Vale.
Make me no Gaudy Chaplet.
My Good Old Darky Home.
My Johnny was a Shoemaker.
Next Election Day.
Nonsense, No.
Nothing More.
Now for a Bully Trip.
Old Friends are Gone.
Poor Old Slave.
Rouse, Brothers, Rouse!
Sally, Come up.
Sally in our Alley.
Sally of the Sewing Machine.
Seeing Nellie Home.
Sweet Virginia Belle.
The Captain with his Whiskers.
The Cove Vot Spouts.
The Dandy Broadway Swell.
The Grave of Uncle True.
The Old Farm Gate.
The Old Sexton.
The Rat-Catcher's Daughter.
The Ring My Mother Wore.
The Shop Gals.
The Sword of Bunker Hill.
The Watchman.
The Woodpecker.
Under the Willow She's Sleeping.
Welcome, Welcome Home.
What Fairy Like Music.
What's Trumps?
Willie Grey; an Answer to Kitty
  Clyde.

Copies mailed to any address, free of postage, upon receipt of Ten Cents.

BRYANT'S ESSENCE OF OLD VIRGINNY.

CONTENTS:

The Bryant Brothers, (*With Eng.*)
The Aristocratic Darkey.
Good bye, John.
New-York City.
The Yaller Gal in the Morning.
The Odder Side of Jordan.
Gay is the Life of a Colored Man.
Adieu, my lovely Georgian Girl.
Blow ye Winds.
Cars are on the Track.
That's so, my Boys.
Down in Alabam, (*With Engraving*)

"Good Bye."
The Bean Law.
The Darkies Sigh.
We are Growing Old.
That's a Pull Back, (*With Eng.*)
Jenny Fair and Bright.
Where can I get a Drink.
Sally Morgan.
Star of the Evening.
Here Now.
Little Log Hut in Old Virginny.
Life on the Farm.

[*Turn Over.*]

Copies mailed to any address, free of Postage, upon receipt of Ten Cents.

UNSWORTH'S BURNT CORK LYRICS.

CONTENTS :

MATT PEEL'S BANJO.

CONTENTS:

Copies mailed to any address, free of postage, upon receipt of Ten Cents.

PETE MORRIS' AMERICAN COMIC MELODIST.

CONTENTS:

[*Turn Over.*]

Copies mailed to any address, free of postage, upon receipt of Ten Cents.

THE RATAPLAN; OR, THE "RED, WHITE AND BLUE" WARBLER.

CONTENTS :

Copies mailed to any address, free of postage, upon receipt of Ten Cents.

THE SOLDIERS' POCKET HEALTH COMPANION, OR, HINTS GATHERED FROM OLD CAMPAIGNERS.

This little work, a copy of which is indispensable to every active Campaigner, has received the commendation of some of the most prominent Military and Medical men, and is designed to supply a vacuum of long standing, and a want of illimitable magnitude.

Copies mailed to any address, free of postage, upon receipt of Ten Cents.

THE ANNIE LAURIE MELODIST.

CONTENTS:

Copies mailed to any address, free of postage, upon receipt of Ten Cents.

PADDY'S OWN DIME SONG BOOK.

CONTENTS:

[Turn Over.]

Copies mailed to any address, free of postage, upon receipt of Ten Cents.

BYRON CHRISTY'S DIME CLOWN JOKE BOOK.

CONTENTS :

Accidental.
Sailing.
A Treasure.
When shall We Three meet again?
Very Wonderful Ink.
A·Valentine.
Pocket Book.
From the Poets.
Curiosities.

Man and Wife One.
Students on a Spree.
Nothing.
I ain't no Sugar Plum.
Fight a la Kansas.
Descriptive.
Wants.
Geographical Examination.

Copies mailed to any address, free of postage, upon receipt of Ten Cents.

THE MAC DILL DARRELL DIME MELODIST.
No. 1.
CONTENTS:

New Mac Dill Darrell.
Root Hog or Die.
The Tyrolese Maid.
Dark Topsey's Song.
No Time to Cry.
She Sleeps in the Grave.
Don't you Hear the Horn a Blowin'.
Poor Hot Corn Girl.
The Negro Band.
Loulie, will you Meet me?
Jim Crow.
Would I were a Girl again.
The Chap that Spouts.
Belinda May.
Sailieur Boy, Nineteen Years Old.
Molly' Bawn.
Old Virginny Rye.
Strike, Boys, Strike!
Jordan am a Hard Road to Trabbel.
The Old Town Crier.
Foreigner's Shanty.
When You and I were Young.
New Jordan—No. 2.
Riding in a "Bus."
New Bobbing Around—No. 1.
Blink-Eyed Josey.
Free and Easy.
The Lucky Coachman.

New Jersey.
Riddle Cum Dink ah Do.
Paddy on the Railroad.
Hoop De Dooden Do.
Machine Poetry.
Mrs. McGraw and Son.
Courtin' Sunday Eve.
Shule, Agra.
The Little Sweep.
Billy was a Bootmaker.
Columbia's Great Glory.
Going out Crabbin'.
Warrior's Tear.
Day and Martin.
Jack Rag.
Fortunate.
The Two Orphans.
The Dead March.
Dennis O'Blarney.
Fall.
Molly Machree.
Season Ticket.
Larry O'Gaff.
Collecting Fruit.
The Irish Boy.
Soliloquy of a Bummer.
The Woodland Maid.
Selling Figs.

Copies mailed to any address, free of postage, upon receipt of Ten Cents.

THE MAC DILL DARRELL DIME MELODIST.
No. 2.
CONTENTS:

Mac Dill Darrell Medley.
What a Curious Fashion.
Fashion of the Times.

Bill of Fare.
My Loulie Dear.
Der Radish Gal.

[Turn Over.]

Copies mailed to any address, free of postage, upon receipt of Ten cents.

NEW DIME AMERICAN JOKER.

CONTENTS :

Copies mailed to any address, free of postage, upon receipt of Ten Cents.

HANDY ANDY SONGSTER.

CONTENTS :

Copies mailed to any address, free of postage, upon receipt of Ten Cents.

www.ingramcontent.com/pod-product-compliance
Lightning Source LLC
Chambersburg PA
CBHW021528270326
41930CB00008B/1143